Year 1 Assessing Pupil Progress in Mathematics (APP)

Photocopiable Activity Book

Introduction

Using the assessment statements outlined on the Primary National Strategy Assessing Pupils Progress Guidelines (reproduced under licence at the beginning of this book) this series of books provides carefully organised assessments for each area of the mathematics curriculum. The activities can be used to determine the level a pupil is working at. They can also be used to indicate gaps in learning.

There is a book for each year group from Year1 – Year 6 aimed at pupils aged 6 to 11. When a written test is completed, an easy to carry out assessment of AT1 (Using and Applying Mathematics) is provided to enable a National Curriculum level to be determined (e.g. Level 3b). The tests are compiled in such a way that a Level 3b would be exactly the same whether achieved on a Y1, Y4 or Y6 assessment.

For each year group there are differentiated assessments aimed at pupils of different abilities.

In this Year 1 book there are assessments for:

Level 1 = Average Ability
Level 2 = Higher Ability
Level 3 = Very High Ability

The assessments within this book can be used as a baseline test or used at the end of a term to assess progress.

Contents

Topical Resources publishes a range of Educational Materials for use in Primary Schools and Pre-School Nurseries and Playgroups.

First Published January 2010.
ISBN: 978-1-907269-17-2

Illustrated by John Hutchinson, Art Works, Fairhaven, 69 Worden Lane, Leyland, Preston

Designed by Paul Sealey, PS3 Creative, 3 Wentworth Drive, Thornton, Lancashire.

Printed in the UK for 'Topical Resources' by T. Snape and Co Ltd., Boltons Court, Preston, Lancashire.

For the latest catalogue
Tel 01772 863158
Fax 01772 866153
email: sales@topical-resources.co.uk

Visit our Website at:
www.topical-resources.co.uk

Mathematics Attainment Target 1 (MA 1) Using and Applying Mathematics

	Problem solving	Communicating	Reasoning
Level 3 (L3)	**A** select the mathematics they use in a wider range of classroom activities, e.g. - *use classroom discussions to break into a problem, recognising similarities to previous work* - *put the problem into their own words* - *use mathematical content from levels 2 and 3* - *choose their own equipment appropriate to the task, including calculators* **B** try different approaches and find ways of overcoming difficulties that arise when they are solving problems, e.g. - *check their work and make appropriate corrections, e.g. decide that two numbers less than 100 cannot give a total more than 200 and correct the addition* - *begin to look for patterns in results as they work and use them to find other possible outcomes*	**A** begin to organise their work and check results, e.g. - *begin to develop own ways of recording* - *develop an organised approach as they get into recording their work on a problem* **B** discuss their mathematical work and begin to explain their thinking, e.g. - *use appropriate mathematical vocabulary* - *talk about their findings by referring to their written work* **C** use and interpret mathematical symbols and diagrams	**A** understand a general statement by finding particular examples that match it, e.g. - *make a generalisation with the assistance of probing questions and prompts* **B** review their work and reasoning, e.g. - *respond to 'What if?' questions* - *when they have solved a problem, pose a similar problem for a partner*
Level 2 (L2)	**A** select the mathematics they use in some classroom activities, e.g. with support - find a starting point, identifying key facts/relevant information - *use apparatus, diagrams, role-play, etc. to represent and clarify a problem* - *move between different representations of a problem, e.g. a situation described in words, a diagram, etc.* - *adopt a suggested model or systematic approach* - *make connections and apply their knowledge to similar situations* - *use mathematical content from levels 1 and 2 to solve problems and investigate*	**A** discuss their work using mathematical language, e.g. with support - *describe the strategies and methods they use in their work* - *engage with others' explanations, compare... evaluate...* **B** begin to represent their work using symbols and simple diagrams, e.g. with support - *use pictures, diagrams and symbols to communicate their thinking, or demonstrate a solution or process* - *begin to appreciate the need to record and develop their own methods of recording*	**A** explain why an answer is correct, e.g. with support - *test a statement such as, 'The number twelve ends with a 2 so 12 sweets can be shared equally by 2 children'* **B** predict what comes next in a simple number, shape or spatial pattern or sequence and give reasons for their opinions of objects, shapes or numbers
Level 1 (L1)	**A** use mathematics as an integral part of classroom activities, e.g. with support - *engage with practical mathematical activities involving sorting, counting and measuring by direct comparison* - *begin to understand the relevance of mathematical ideas to everyday situations by using them in role-play*	**A** represent their work with objects or pictures **B** discuss their work, e.g. with support - *respond to questions and ideas from peers and adults* - *refer to the materials they have used and talk about what they have done, patterns they have noticed, etc.*	**A** draw simple conclusions from their work, e.g. with support - *describe the different ways they have sorted objects, what is the same about objects in a set, how sets differ* - *identify which set has most, which object is biggest, smallest, tallest, etc.* - *explain numbers and calculations, how many altogether, how many used or hidden, how many left, how many each, etc.* **B** recognise and use a simple pattern or relationship, e.g. with support - copy and continue a simple pattern of objects, shapes or numbers

Mathematics Attainment Target 2 (MA 2) Number and Algebra

Level 3 (L3)	Numbers & the number system	Fractions and decimals	Operations, relationships....	Mental methods	Solving numerical problems	Written methods
	A understand place value in numbers to 1000, e.g. *- represent/compare numbers using number lines, 100-squares, base 10 materials, etc.* *- recognise that some numbers can be represented as different arrays* *- use understanding of place value to multiply/divide whole numbers by 10 (whole number answers)* **B** use place value to make approximations **C** recognise negative numbers in contexts such as temperature **D** recognise a wider range of sequences, e.g. *- recognise sequences of multiples of 2, 5 and 10*	**A** use simple fractions that are several parts of a whole and recognise when two simple fractions are equivalent, e.g. *- understand and use unit fractions such as 1/2, 1/4, 1/3, 1/5, 1/10 and find those fractions of shapes and sets of objects* *- recognise and record fractions that are several parts of the whole such as 3/4, 2/5* *- recognise some fractions that are equivalent to 1/2* **B** begin to use decimal notation in contexts such as money, e.g. - order decimals with one dp, or two dp in context of money - know that £3.06 equals 306p	**A** derive associated division facts from known multiplication facts, e.g. *- given a number sentence, use understanding of operations to create related sentences, e.g. given 14 × 5 = 70, create 5 × 14 = 70, 70 ÷ 5 = 14, 70 ÷ 14 = 5, 14 × 5 = 10 × 5 add 4 × 5* *- use inverses to find missing whole numbers in problems such as 'I think of a number, double it and add 5. The answer is 35. What was my number?'* **B** begin to understand the role of '=', the 'equals' sign, e.g. *- solve 'balancing' problems such as 7 × 10 = 82 - __*	**A** add and subtract two-digit numbers mentally, e.g. *- calculate 36 + 19, 63 - 26, and complements to 100 such as 100 - 24* **B** use mental recall of the 2, 3, 4, 5 and 10 multiplication tables, e.g. *- multiply a two-digit number by 2, 3, 4 or 5* *- understand finding a quarter of a number of objects as halving the number and halving again* *- begin to know multiplication facts for ×6, ×8, ×9 and ×7 tables*	**A** use mental recall of addition and subtraction facts to 20 in solving problems involving larger numbers, e.g. *- choose to calculate mentally, on paper or with apparatus* *- solve one-step whole number problems appropriately* *- solve two-step problems that involve addition and subtraction* **B** solve whole number problems including those involving multiplication or division that may give rise to remainders, e.g. *- identify appropriate operations to use* *- round up or down after simple division, depending on context*	**A** add and subtract three digit numbers using written method, e.g. *- use written methods that involve bridging 10 or 100* *- add and subtract decimals in the context of money, where bridging is not required* **B** multiply and divide two digit numbers by 2, 3, 4 or 5 as well as 10 with whole number answers and remainders, e.g. *- calculate 49 ÷ 3*

Level 2 (L2)	Numbers & the number system	Fractions	Operations, relationships....	Mental methods	Solving numerical problems	Written methods
	A count sets of objects reliably, e.g. *- group objects in tens, twos or fives to count them* **B** begin to understand the place value of each digit, use this to order numbers up to 100, e.g. *- know the relative size of numbers to 100* *- use 0 as a place holder* *- demonstrate knowledge using a range of models/images* **C** recognise sequences of numbers, including odd and even numbers, e.g. *- continue a sequence that increases or decreases in regular steps* *- recognise numbers from counting in tens or twos*	**A** begin to use halves and quarters, e.g. *- use the concept of a fraction of a small quantity in a practical context such as sharing sweets between two and getting ½ each, among four and getting ¼ each* *- work out halves of numbers up to 20 and beginning to recall them* **B** relate the concept of half of a small quantity to the concept of half of a shape, e.g. *- shade one half or one quarter of a given shape including those divided*	**A** use the knowledge that subtraction is the inverse of addition, e.g. *- begin to understand subtraction as 'difference'* *- given 14, 6 and 8, make related number sentences 6 + 8 = 14, 14 - 8 = 6, 8 + 6 = 14, 14 - 6 = 8* **B** understand halving as a way of 'undoing' doubling and vice versa	**A** use mental recall of addition and subtraction facts to 10, e.g. *- use addition/subtraction facts to 10 and place value to add or subtract multiples of 10, e.g. know 3 + 7 = 10 and use place value to derive 30 + 70 = 100.* **B** use mental calculation strategies to solve number problems including those involving money and measures, e.g. *- recall doubles to 10 + 10 and other significant doubles, e.g. double 50p is 100p or £1* *- use knowledge of doubles to 10 + 10 to derive corresponding halves*	**A** choose the appropriate operation when solving addition and subtraction problems *- use repeated addition to solve multiplication problems* *- begin to use repeated subtraction or sharing equally to solve division problems* **B** solve number problems involving money and measures, e.g. *- add/subtract two-digit and onedigit numbers, bridging tens where necessary in contexts using units such as pence, pounds, centimetres*	**A** record their work in writing, e.g. *- record their mental calculations as number sentences*

Level 1 (L1)	Numbers & the number system	Fractions	Operations, relationships....	Mental methods	Solving numerical problems	Written methods
	A count up to 10 objects, e.g. *- estimate and check a number* **B** read, write numbers to 10 *- perhaps with some reversal* **C** order numbers to 10 *- say what number comes next, is one more/less* *- count back to zero* *- place 1-10 into ascending order* *- point to first, second, etc. in a line* *- begin to count in twos*	**A** begin to use the fraction, one-half, e.g. *- halve shapes including folding paper shapes, lengths of string* *- put water in a clear container so that it is about 'half-full'* *- halve an even number of objects*	**A** understand addition as finding the total of two or more sets of objects **B** understand subtraction as 'taking away' objects from a set and finding	**A** add and subtract numbers of objects to 10 *- begin to add by counting on from the number of objects in the first set* **B** begin to know some addition facts, e.g. *- doubles of numbers to double 5*	**A** solve addition/subtraction problems involving up to 10 objects, e.g. *- given a number work out 'how many more to make…'* *- choose which of given pairs of numbers add to a given total* *- solve measuring problems such as how many balance with…* *- solve problems involving 1p or £1 coins*	**A** record their work, e.g. *- record their work with objects, pictures or diagrams* *- begin to use the symbols '+' and '=' to record L1 additions*

Mathematics Attainment Target 3 (MA 3) Shape, Space and Measures

	Properties of shape	Properties of position and movement	Measures
Level 3 (L3)	**A** classify 3-D and 2-D shapes in various ways using mathematical properties such as reflective symmetry for 2-D shapes, e.g. - *sort objects and shapes using more than one criterion, e.g. pentagon, not pentagon and all edges the same length/not the same length* - *sort the shapes which have all edges the same length and all angles the same size from a set of mixed shapes and begin to understand the terms 'regular' and 'irregular'* - *recognise right angles in shapes in different orientations* - *recognise angles which are bigger/smaller than 90° and begin to know the terms 'obtuse' and 'acute'* - *recognise right-angled and equilateral triangles* - *demonstrate that a shape has reflection symmetry by folding and recognise when a shape does not have a line of symmetry* - *recognise common 3-D shapes, e.g. triangular prism, square-based pyramid* - *relate 3-D shapes to drawings and photographs of them, including from different viewpoints* **B** begin to recognise nets of familiar 3-D shapes, e.g. cube, cuboid, triangular prism, square-based pyramid	**A** recognise shapes in different orientations **B** reflect shapes, presented on a grid, in a vertical or horizontal mirror line, e.g. - *reflect a shape even if the shape is at 45° to the mirror line, touching the line or not* - *begin to reflect simple shapes in a mirror line presented at 45°* **C** describe position and movement, e.g. - *use terms such as left/right, clockwise/anticlockwise, quarter turn/90° to give directions along a route*	**A** use non-standard units and standard metric units of length, capacity and mass in a range of contexts, e.g. - *measure a length to the nearest 1/2 cm* - *read simple scales, e.g. increments of 2, 5 or 10* **B** use standard units of time, e.g. - *read a 12-hour clock and generally calculate time durations that do not go over the hour* **C** use a wider range of measures, e.g. - *begin to understand area as a measure of surface and perimeter as a measure of length* - *begin to find areas of shapes by counting squares and explain answers as a number of squares even if not using standard units such as cm^2 or m^2* - *recognise angles as a measure of turn and know that one whole turn is 360 degrees*
	Properties of shape	**Properties of position and movement**	**Measures**
Level 2 (L2)	**A** use mathematical names for common 3-D and 2-D shapes, e.g. - *identify 2-D and 3-D shapes from pictures of them in different orientations, e.g. square, triangle, hexagon, pentagon, octagon, cube, cylinder, sphere, cuboid, pyramid* **B** describe their properties, including numbers of sides and corners, e.g. - *make and talk about shapes referring to features and properties using language such as edge, face, corner* - *sort 2-D and 3-D shapes according to a single criterion, e.g. shapes that are pentagons or shapes with a right angle* - *visualise frequently used 2-D and 3-D shapes* - *begin to understand the difference between shapes with two dimensions and those with three* - *recognise the properties that are the same even when a shape is enlarged, e.g. when comparing squares, circles, similar triangles, cubes or spheres of different sizes*	**A** describe the position of objects, e.g. - *use ordinal numbers (first, second, third…) to describe the position of objects in a row or when giving directions* - *recognise and explain that a shape stays the same even when it is held up in different orientations* **B** distinguish between straight and turning movements - *distinguish between left and right and between clockwise and anticlockwise and use these when giving directions* - *instruct a programmable robot, combining straight-line movements and turns, to move along a defined path or reach a target destination* **C** recognise right angles in turns	**A** understand angle as a measurement of turn - *make whole turns, half turns and quarter turns* **B** begin to use everyday non-standard and standard units to measure length and mass - *begin to understand that numbers can be used not only to count discrete objects but also to describe continuous measures, e.g. length* - *know which measuring tools to use to find, for example, how much an object weighs, how tall a child is, how long it takes to run around the edge of the playground, how much water it takes to fill the water tray* - *read scales to the nearest labelled division - begin to make sensible estimates in relation to familiar units* **C** begin to use a wider range of measures - *make and use a 'right angle checker'* - *use a time line to order daily events and ordinal numbers (first, second, third…) to describe the order of some regular events*
	Properties of shape	**Properties of position and movement**	**Measures**
Level 1 (L1)	**A** use everyday language to describe properties of 2-D and 3-D shapes, e.g. - *sort shapes and say how they have selected them* - *use properties such as large, small, triangles, roll, stack* - *begin to refer to some features of shapes such as side and corner* - *begin to name the shapes they use in the context of an activity*	**A** use everyday language to describe positions of 2-D and 3-D shapes - *respond to and use positional language, e.g. 'behind', under', 'on top of', 'next to', 'in between'…* - *respond to and use directional language in talk about objects and movement, e.g. 'forwards', 'backwards', 'turn'*	**A** measure and order objects using direct comparison - *compare lengths directly and put them in order* - *respond to and use the language of comparison: longer, longest, shorter, shortest, more, less, heavier, lighter* - *check which of two objects is heavier/lighter and begin to put three objects into order* - *find objects that are longer/shorter than a metre, heavier/lighter than 500 grams, hold more/less than 1 litre* **B** order events - *order everyday events and describe the sequence* - *use the vocabulary of time including days of the week* - *read the time on an analogue clock at the hour and begin to know the half hour*

Mathematics Attainment Target 4 (MA 4) Handling Data

	Processing and representing data	Interpreting data
Level 3 (L3)	**A** gather information, e.g. *- decide what data to collect to answer a question, e.g. what is the most common way to travel to school* *- make appropriate choices for recording data, e.g. a tally chart or frequency table* **B** construct bar charts and pictograms, where the symbol represents a group of units, e.g. *- decide how best to represent data, e.g. whether a bar chart, Venn diagram or pictogram would show the information most clearly* *- decide upon an appropriate scale for a graph, e.g. labelled divisions of 2, or, for a pictogram, one symbol to represent 2 or 5* **C** use Venn and Carroll diagrams to record their sorting and classifying of information, e.g. *- represent sorting using one or two criteria typical of level 2 and 3 mathematics, e.g. shapes sorted using properties such as right angles and equal sides*	**A** extract and interpret information presented in simple tables, lists, bar charts and pictograms, e.g. *- use a key to interpret represented data* *- read scales labelled in twos, fives and tens, including reading between labelled divisions such as a point halfway between 40 and 50 or 8 and 10* *- compare data, e.g. say how many more… than… and recognise the category that has most/least* *- respond to questions of a more complex nature such as 'How many children took part in this survey altogether?' or 'How would the data differ if we asked the children in Year 6?'* *- in the context of data relating to everyday situations, understand the idea of 'certain' and 'impossible' relating to probability*

	Processing and representing data	Interpreting data
Level 2 (L2)	**A** sort objects and classify them using more than one criterion, e.g. *- sort a given set of shapes using two criteria such as triangle/not triangle and blue/not blue* **B** understand vocabulary relating to handling data, e.g. *- understand vocabulary such as sort, group, set, list, table, most common, most popular* **C** collect and sort data to test a simple hypothesis, e.g. *- count a show of hands to test the hypothesis 'most children in our class are in bed by7:30pm'* **D** record results in simple lists, tables, pictograms and block graphs, e.g. *- present information in lists, tables and simple graphs where one symbol or block represents one unit* *- enter data into a simple computer database*	**A** communicate their findings, using the simple lists, tables, pictograms and block graphs they have recorded, e.g. *- respond to questions about the data they have presented, e.g. how many of our names have 5 letters?* *- pose similar questions about their data for others to answer*

	Processing and representing data	Interpreting data
Level 1 (L1)	**A** sort and classify objects, e.g. *- sort using one criterion or sort into disjoint sets using two simple criteria such as boy/girl or thick/thin* *- sort objects again using a different criterion* *- sort objects into a given large scale Venn or Carroll diagram* **B** represent their work, e.g. *- use the objects they have sorted as a record* *- use objects/pictures to create simple block graphs*	**A** demonstrate the criterion they have used, e.g. *- respond to questions about how they have sorted objects and why each object belongs in a set* *- talk about which set has most, for example 'most children stayed at school for lunch'* *- talk about how they have represented their work*

Assessing Pupil Progress in Mathematics (APP)
and Identifying Gaps in Pupil's Learning (Year 1 - Level 1)

Name [ ] Date [ ]

This test can be used to confirm a teacher's informal assessment of a pupil. It can also be used to indicate gaps in a pupil's learning.

How to confirm a teacher's informal assessment of a pupil
The test is in two parts. One part consists of an un-timed assessment which needs to be carried out in a one-to-one small group situation. (N.B. For less able childen this activity may take longer than one sitting.) The other part (found below) consists of a simple grid for the teacher to complete after observing the pupil in a normal classroom situation. This part of the assessment mainly indicates performance against Attainment Target 1 – Using and Applying Mathematics. The scores for the two tests should be added together and a National Curriculum sub-level awarded using the information in the table at the bottom of this page. The resulting score should give a clear indication of which sub-level the pupil is working at within the levels found in the English National Curriculum.

How to indicate gaps in a pupil's learning
Each question on the written paper is accompanied by the learning objective it represents taken from the tables reproduced at the beginning of the book. By referring to the incorrect questions a list of learning objectives which indicate the gaps in the pupil's learning can quickly and easily be made up.

Teacher Assessment of Attainment Target 1 – Using & Applying (Ma1) 2 marks indicates competent 1 mark indicates some ability 0 mark indicates unable to carry out	**Mark** 0,1 or 2 for each statement
Ma1/L1 – Problem solving - Part A Use mathematics as an integral part of classroom activities	
Ma1/L1 – Communicating - Part A Represent their work with objects or pictures	
Ma1/L1 – Communicating - Part B Discuss their work	
Ma1/L1 – Reasoning - Part A Draw simple conclusions from their work	
Ma1/L1 – Reasoning - Part B Recognise and use a simple pattern or relationship	
Total =	

	Actual	**Possible**
Total AT1		10
Total Activities		50
Total		60
Level		

Level 1a high = 50 - 60

Level 1b secure = 35 - 49

Level 1c low = 21 - 34

Below Level 1 = 20 or less

Ma 2 Number and Algebra page 1 of 3

Name

Date

	Practitioner:	Ask child:	Mark	Marks Available	APP statement	Reference
1.	Point to the owls (Resource Page 4a).	How many owls are there?		1	**Count up to 10 objects** *Estimate and check a number*	***Ma2/L1 - Numbers and the number system - Part A***
2.	Point to the dogs (Resource Page 4b).	How many dogs are there?		1	**Count up to 10 objects** *Estimate and check a number*	***Ma2/L1 - Numbers and the number system - Part A***
3.	Give the child a piece of paper and a pencil.	Write number 7, *wait for child to write.* Write number 9, *wait for child to write.* Write number 3, *wait for child to write.* Write number 8, *wait for child to write.* Write number 1, *wait for child to write.* Write number 4, *wait for child to write.* Write number 2, *wait for child to write.* Write number 5, *wait for child to write.* Write number 10, *wait for child to write.* Write number 6, *wait for child to write.*		8 to 10 numbers correct **2 marks** 6 or 7 numbers correct **1 mark**	**Read, write numbers to 10** *Perhaps with some reversals*	***Ma2/L1 - Numbers and the number system - Part B***
4.	Show the number 6 (Resource Page 4c).	This is number 6. What number comes next?		1	**Order numbers to 10** *Say what number comes next*	***Ma2/L1 - Numbers and the number system - Part C***
5.	Show the number 5 (Resource Page 4d).	This is number 5. What number is one more than 5?		1	**Order numbers to 10** *Say what number is one more*	***Ma2/L1 - Numbers and the number system - Part C***
6.	Show the number 8 (Resource Page 4e).	This is number 8. What number is one less than 8?		1	**Order numbers to 10** *Say what number is one less*	***Ma2/L1 - Numbers and the number system - Part C***
7.	*Show the numbers 10, 9* (Resource Page 4f).	*Start at number 10 for me and count backward*		1 encourage to keep counting back until s/he reaches 0.	**Order numbers to 10** *Count back to 0*	***Ma2/L1 - Numbers and the number system - Part C***
8.	*Give child numbers 1 - 10* (cut out from resource Page 1).	Put these numbers in order for me.		1	**Order numbers to 10** *Place 1 – 10 into ascending order*	***Ma2/L1 - Numbers and the number system - Part C***
9.	Show the row of shapes (Resource page 5g).	Look at the shapes – point to the 5th one.		1	**Order numbers to 10** *Point to 1st, 2nd etc in a line*	***Ma2/L1 - Numbers and the number system - Part C***
10.	Show the child the row of numbers. (Resource Page 5h).	Listen carefully and tell me what are the next two numbers – 2,4,6.		1	**Order numbers to 10** *Begin to count in twos*	***Ma2/L1 - Numbers and the number system - Part C***

Ma 2 Number and Algebra page 2 of 3

Name

Date

	Practitioner:	Ask child:	Mark	Marks Available	APP statement	Reference
11.	Give the child a piece of A4 paper.	Please can you fold this piece of paper in half.		1	**Begin to use the fraction one-half** *Halve shapes including folding paper shapes and lengths of string*	***Ma2/L1 – Fractions – Part A***
12.	Give the child a glass and a jug of water.	Please can you pour some water into the class so that it is half-full.		1	**Begin to use the fraction one-half** *Put water in a clear container so that is about 'half-full'*	***Ma2/L1 – Fractions – Part A***
13.	Show the child the flowers (Resource page 5i).	Here are some flowers. Can you tell me how many is half of the flowers?		1	**Begin to use the fraction one-half** *Halve an even number of objects*	***Ma2/L1 – Fractions – Part A***
14.	Put out 4 bears in one pile, 3 bears in another pile and 2 in another pile.	There are 4 bears here (point), 3 bears here (point) and 2 bears (point) here. How many is that altogether? You can touch the bears if you wish.		1	**Understand addition as finding the total of two or more sets of objects**	***Ma2/L1 - Operations, relationships between them – Part A***
15.	Put out 7 bears.	Here are 7 bears, if I take away 3, how many are left? You can touch the bears if you wish.		1	**Understand subtraction as 'taking away' objects from a set and finding out how many are left**	***Ma2/L1 - Operations, relationships between them – Part B***
16.	Show the child the sum (ResourcePage 5j).	What is 3 add 4?		1	**Add and subtract numbers of objects to 10** *Begin to add by counting on from the number of objects in the first set*	***Ma2/L1 - Mental Methods – Part A***
17.		*What is 2 + 2* *What is 5 + 5* *What is 3 + 3* *What is 1 + 1* *What is 4 + 4*		*All Correct* ***3 marks*** *3 or 4 answers correct* ***2 marks*** *2 answers correct* ***1 mark***	**Begin to know some addition facts** *Doubles of numbers to double 5*	***Ma2/L1 - Mental Methods – Part B***

Ma 2 Number and Algebra page 3 of 3

Name | Date

	Practitioner:	Ask child:	Mark	Marks Available	APP statement	Reference
18.	Put out 3 bears.	If I have 3 bears, how many more make 5?		1	**Solve addition/subtraction problems involving up to 10 objects** *Given a number, work out how many more make ...*	***Ma2/L1 - Solving Numerical Problems – Part A***
19.	Show the child the sums (Resource Page 5k).	Can you point to the pair that makes 9?		1	**Solve addition/subtraction problems involving up to 10 objects** *Choose which of given pairs of numbers add up to a given total* Ma2/L1 - Solving Numerical	***Ma2/L1 - Solving Numerical Problems – Part A***
20.	Put the banana on the balance.	Ask the child to use the conkers to work out how many balance with the banana.		1	**Solve addition/subtraction problems involving up to 10 objects** *Solve measuring problems such as how many balance with ...*	***Ma2/L1 - Solving Numerical Problems – Part A***
21.	Show the child the money (7 x 1p coins).	How much money do I had here?		1	**Solve addition/subtraction problems involving up to 10 objects** *Solve problems involving 1p or £1 coins*	***Ma2/L1 - Solving Numerical Problems – Part A***
22.	Give the child a piece of paper and a pencil.	There are 5 balls and I get 3 more – can you draw this for me?		1	**Record their work** *Record their work with objects, pictures of diagrams*	***Ma2/L1 - Written Methods – Part A***
23.	Give the child a piece of paper and a pencil.	I am going to say a sum. Can you write it down with numbers and signs? Four add four equals eight.		1	**Record their work** *Begin to use the symbols '+' and '=' to record additions*	***Ma2/L1 - Written Methods – Part A***

Ma 3 Shape, Space & Measures page 1 of 2

Name

Date

	Practitioner:	Ask child:	Mark	Marks Available	APP statement	Reference
24.	Give the child the following shapes: Circle, triangle, square and rectangle (one small and one large).	Can you sort these shapes into two groups? Why did you sort them like that?		1	**Use everyday language to describe properties of 2-D and 3-D shapes** *Sort shapes and say how they have been selected*	***Ma3 - Properties of shape – Part A***
25.	Give the child a cylinder. Give the child 6 squares.	Can you roll the cylinder to me? Can you stack the squares?		1	**Use everyday language to describe properties of 2-D and 3-D shapes** *Use properties such as large, small, triangles, roll, stack*	***Ma3 - Properties of shape – Part A***
26.	Point to the triangle.	Look at this shape – how many sides does it have?		1	**Use everyday language to describe properties of 2-D and 3-D shapes** *Begin to refer to some feature of shapes such as side and corner*	***Ma3 - Properties of shape – Part A***
27.	Point to the triangle again.	What is the name of this shape?		1	**Use everyday language to describe properties of 2-D and 3-D shapes** *Begin to name the shapes they use in the context of an activity*	***Ma3 - Properties of shape – Part A***
28.	Give the child the cuddly teddy.	Put the bear 'behind' you Put the bear 'under' the table Put the bear 'on top of the table', Put the bear 'next to' me Put the bear 'in between' me and you!		1 (1 mistake can be made)	**Use everyday language to describe positions of 2-D and 3-D shapes** Respond to and use positional language e.g. 'behind', 'under', 'on top of', 'next to', 'in between'	***Ma3 - Properties of position and movement – Part A***
29.	Tell the child to listen carefully because you are going to ask them to follow some instructions.	Stand up. Walk forwards. Walk backwards. Turn for me.		1	**Use everyday language to describe positions of 2-D and 3-D shapes** *Respond to and use directional language in talk about objects and movements e.g. 'forwards', 'backwards', 'turn'*	***Ma3 - Properties of position and movement – Part A***

Ma 3 Shape, Space & Measures page 1 of 2

Name ______ Date ______

	Practitioner:	Ask child:	Mark	Marks Available	APP statement	Reference
30.	Give the 3 strips of paper (cut out from Resource Page 2).	Put these strips in order. shortest first and longest last.		1	**Measure and order objects using direct comparison** *compare lengths directly and put them in order*	*Ma3/L1 – Measures – Part A*
31.	Give the 3 strips of paper (cut out from Resource Page 2).	Which is the shortest strip?		1	**Measure and order objects using direct comparison** *respond to and use the language of comparison: longer, longest, shorter, shortest, more,less, heavier, lighter.*	*Ma3/L1 – Measures – Part A*
32.	Give the child two objects.	Which object is heavier?		1	**Measure and order objects using direct comparison** *- check which of two objects is heavier/lighter and begin to put three objects into order*	*Ma3 - Properties of shape – Part A*
33.		Can you tell me something that is longer than a metre? Can you tell me something is lighter than 500g? Can you tell me something that holds less than 1 litre?		3	**Measure and order objects using direct comparison** *find objects that are longer/shorter than a metre-, heavier/lighter than 500 grams, hold more/less than 1 litre*	*Ma3/L1 – Measures – Part A*
34.	Give child the 6 pictures (cut out from Resource Page 2).	Which did you do first today? Can you put the other pictures in order?		1	**Order Events** *- order everyday events and describe the sequence*	*Ma3/L1 – Measures – Part B*
35.		What day is it today? What day is it tomorrow?		1	**Order Events** *- use the vocabulary of time including days of the week*	*Ma3/L1 – Measures – Part B*
36.	Using the teaching clock, show the child three o'clock. Show the child half past 7.	What time does the clock say? What time does the clock say?		1	**Order Events** *read the time on an analogue clock at the hour and begin to know the half hour*	*Ma3/L1 – Measures – Part B*

Ma 4 Handling Data page 1 of 2

Name

Date

	Practitioner:	Ask child:	Mark	Marks Available	APP statement	Reference
37.	Show the child resource page 6 and give them the pictures of children cut out from Resource Page 3.	Can you sort the children into boys and girls.		1	**Sort and Classify objects** *Sort using one criterion or sort into disjoint sets using two simple criteria such as boy/girl or thick/thin*	***Ma4/L1 - Processing and representing data – Part A***
38.	Take the pictures off the paper.	Can you sort the children in a different way?		1	**Sort and Classify objects** *Sort objects again using a different criterion*	***Ma4/L1 - Processing and representing data – Part A***
39.	Point at the pictures.	Why did you put them into this square?		1	**Demonstrate the criterion they have used** *Respond to questions about how they have sorted objects and why each object belongs in a set*	***Ma4/L1 - Interpreting data – Part A***
40.	Point to their sorting.	Which set has the most children?		1	**Demonstrate the criterion they have used** *Talk about which set has most, for example most children stayed at school for lunch*	***Ma4/L1 - Interpreting data – Part A***
41.	Pointing to a specific child in the sorting (a girl).	Can you tell me why you put this girl in this square?		1	**Demonstrate the criterion they have used** *Talk about how they have represented their work*	***Ma4/L1 - Interpreting data – Part A***
42.	Give the child Resource Page 7 and a red square. Read the headings for the child	Can you put this red square on the venn diagram?		1	**Sort and Classify objects** *Sort objects into a given large scale Venn or Carroll diagram*	***Ma4/L1 - Processing and representing data – Part A***
43	Give the child Resource Page 8 and a red square. Read the headings for the child.	Can you put this red square on the Carroll diagram?		1	**Sort and Classify objects** *Sort objects into a given large scale Venn or Carroll diagram*	***Ma4/L1 - Processing and representing data – Part A***
44.	Give the child Resource Page 8 and the pictures of animals from Resource Page 3. Read the labels on the graph.	Can you make a graph using these animals?		1	**Represent their work** *Use objects/pictures to create simple block graphs*	***Ma4/L1 - Processing and representing data – Part B***
45.		This is a graph to show how many children like different animals. How many children like dogs?		1	**Represent their work** *Use the objects they have sorted as a record*	***Ma4/L1 - Processing and representing data – Part B***

Teacher Resource Sheets – Y1 (Level 1)

You will also need to provide

- 6 pieces of A4 paper
- A pencil for the child to write with
- 10 bears for children to count with
- 1 teddy bear
- A glass and jug of water
- A balancing scale, a banana and some conkers
- 7 x 1p coins
- A cylinder, 6 squares and one triangle
- 2 objects – one that feels quite heavy, the other quite light (e.g. a cricket ball and a hollow ball)
- A teaching clock
- A red square

Before carrying out the assessment, you will need to cut out the resources on the next 3 pages and print out the resource sheets

Photocopy the numbers below, then cut out singly.

1	2	3	4	5
6	7	8	9	10

Photocopy the strips below, then cut out singly.

Photocopy the pictures below, then cut out singly.

Photocopy the pictures below, then cut out singly.

Photocopy the pictures below, then cut out singly.

(a)

(b)

(c) 6

(d) 5

(e) 8

(f) 10, 9 ....

(g)

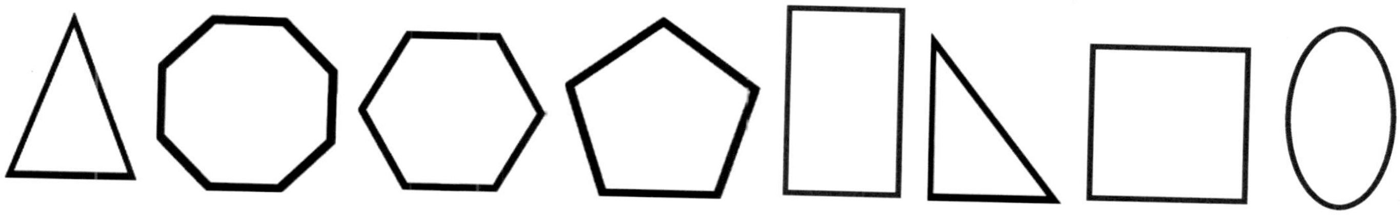

(h) 2, 4, 6 ....

(i)

(j) 3 + 4 =

(k) 3 + 2 =

3 + 5 =

3 + 6 =

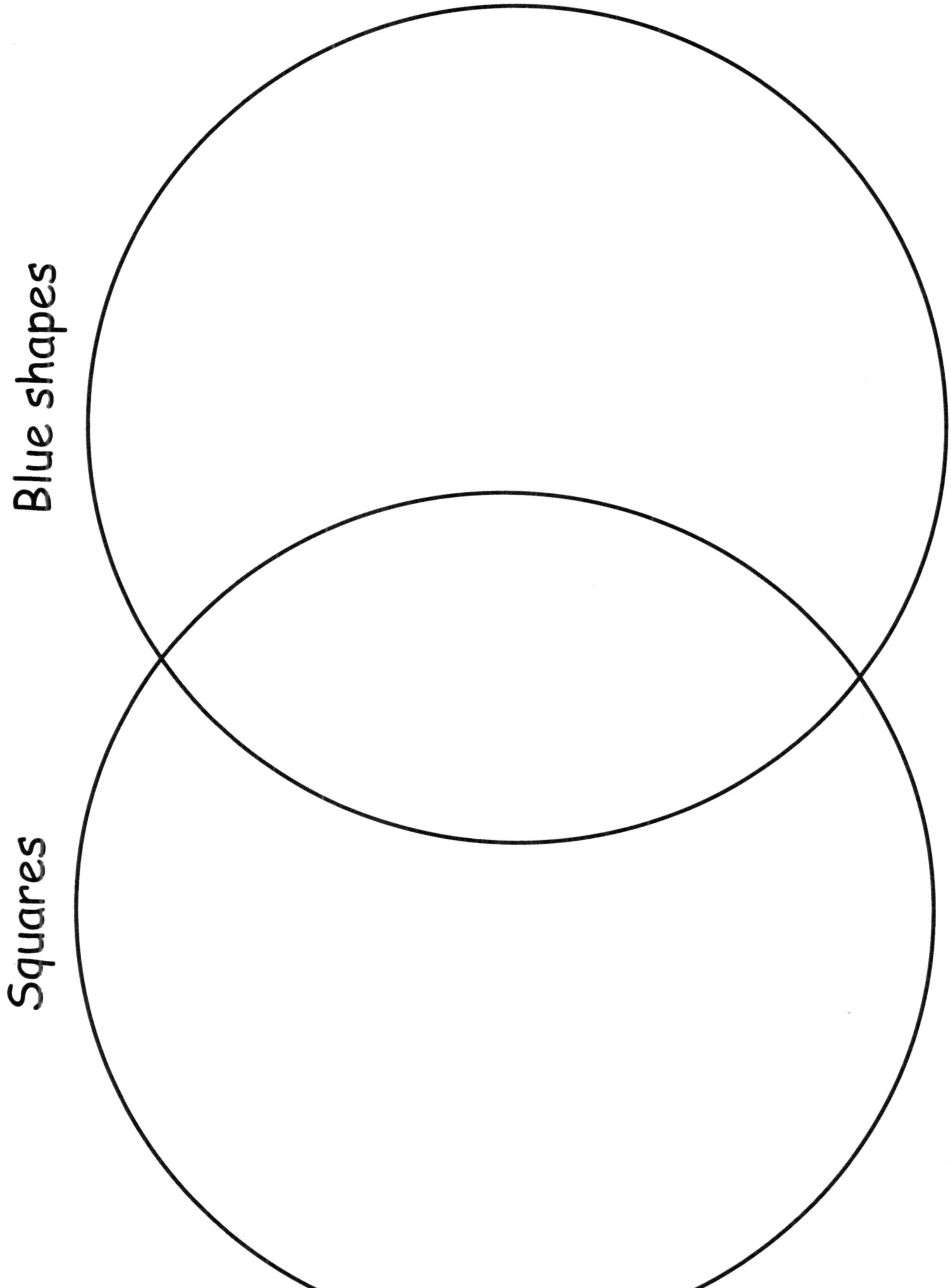
Blue shapes
Squares

	Red	Not Red
Triangle		
Not Triangle		

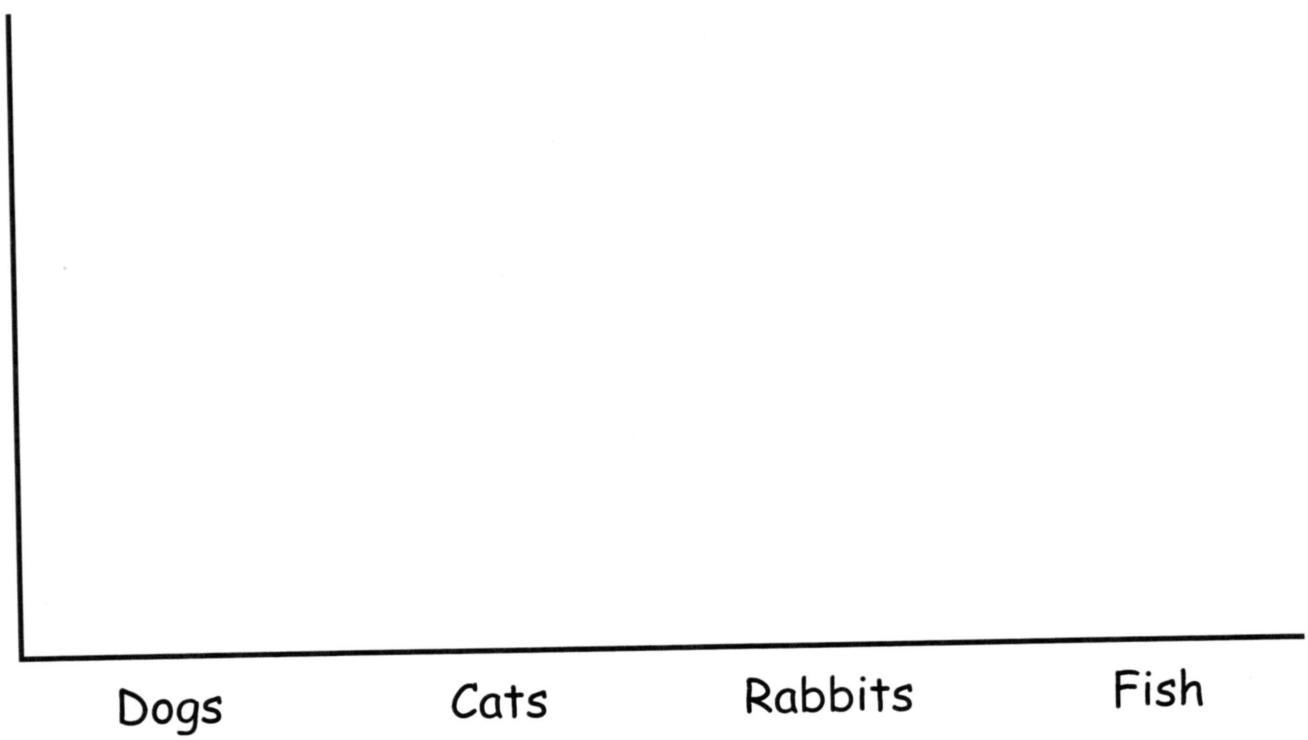

Assessing Pupil Progress in Mathematics (APP)
and Identifying Gaps in Pupil's Learning (Year 1 - Level 2)

Name ____________ Date ____________

This test can be used to confirm a teacher's informal assessment of a pupil. It can also be used to indicate gaps in a pupil's learning.

How to confirm a teacher's informal assessment of a pupil

The test is in two parts. One part consists of an un-timed written paper test for the pupil to complete unaided. The other part (found below) consists of a simple grid for the teacher to complete after observing the pupil in a normal classroom situation. This part of the assessment mainly indicates performance against Attainment Target 1 – Using and Applying Mathematics. The scores for the two tests should be added together and a National Curriculum sub-level awarded using the information in the table at the bottom of this page. The resulting score should give a clear indication of which sub-level the pupil is working at within the levels found in the English National Curriculum.

How to indicate gaps in a pupil's learning

Each question on the written paper is accompanied by the learning objective it represents taken from the tables reproduced at the beginning of the book. By referring to the incorrect questions a list of learning objectives which indicate the gaps in the pupil's learning can quickly and easily be made up.

Teacher Assessment of Attainment Target 1 – Using & Applying (Ma1) and some of Attainment Target 4 – Handling and Data (Ma4) 2 marks indicates competent 1 mark indicates some ability 0 mark indicates unable to carry out	**Mark** 0,1 or 2 for each statement
Ma1/L2 – Problem solving - Part A Select the mathematics they use in some classroom activities, e.g. with support – find a starting point, identifying key	
Ma1/L2 – Communicating - Part A Discuss their work using mathematical language	
Ma1/L2 – Communicating - Part B Begin to represent their work using symbols and simple diagrams	
Ma1/L4 – Reasoning - Part A Explain why an answer is correct	
Ma1/L2 – Reasoning - Part B Predict what comes next in a simple number, shape or spatial pattern or sequence and give reasons for their opinions of	
Total =	

	Actual	**Possible**
Teacher Assessment of AT1 from above.		10
Paper Test Score		40
Total		50
Sub Level Awarded		

Level 2a high	**= 42 - 50**
Level 2b secure	**= 32 - 41**
Level 2c low	**= 21 - 31**
Below Level 2	**= 20 or less**

1. How many footprints are there altogether?

footprints

Ma2/L2
Numbers and the number system Part A

Count sets of objects reliably

1 mark

Look at these numbers.

35 78 71 19 81

2. Write down the largest number.

3. Write down the smallest number.

Ma2/L2
Numbers and the number system Part B

Begin to understand the place value of each digit; use this to order numbers up to 100

2 marks

4. Write the next two numbers in this sequence.

16	26	36		

Teacher's notes

Ma2/L2
Numbers and the number system
Part C

Recognise sequences of numbers, including odd and even numbers

1 mark

---

5. Tick the boxes that have an even number inside them.

51	9	12	6	23
3	2	17	0	40

Ma2/L2
Numbers and the number system
Part C

Recognise sequences of numbers, including odd and even numbers

1 mark

6. If Isabella ate half of the strawberries, how many did she eat?

strawberries

Ma2/L2
Fractions
Part A

Begin to use halves and quarters

1 mark

---

7. If Frahey ate a quarter of the strawberries, how many did she eat?

strawberries

Ma2/L2
Fractions
Part A

Begin to use halves and quarters

1 mark

---

8. What is half of 12?

Ma2/L2
Fractions
Part A

Begin to use halves and quarters

1 mark

---

9. What is half of 6?

Ma2/L2
Fractions
Part A

Begin to use halves and quarters

1 mark

Teacher's notes

10. Colour in a half of this shape.

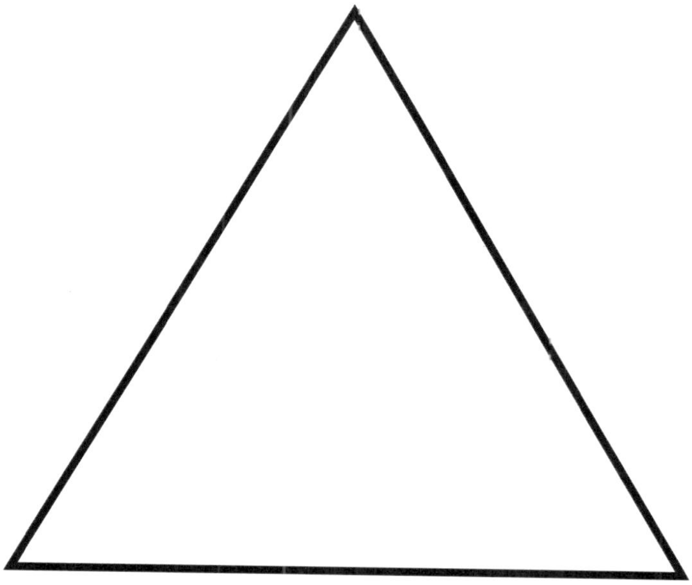

11. Colour in a quarter of this shape.

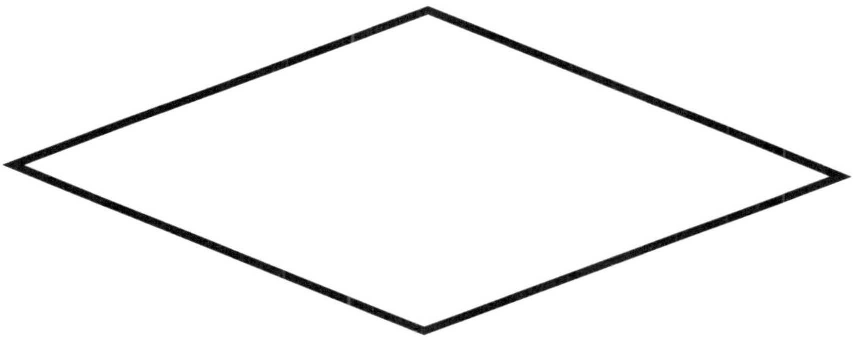

12. Find the difference between 10 and 4.

Teacher's notes

Ma2/L2
Fractions
Part B

Relate the concept of half of a small quantity to the concept of half of a shape

1 mark

Ma2/L2
Fractions
Part B

Relate the concept of half of a small quantity to the concept of half of a shape

1 mark

Ma2/L2
Operations, relationships between them
Part A

Use the knowledge that subtraction is the inverse of addition

1 mark

13. Use 10 + 8 = 18 to make two different take away sentences.

So 18 - ☐ = ☐

and 18 - ☐ = ☐

---

14. Find half and double of each number in the middle.

Half		Double
2	4	8
5	10	☐
☐	12	☐
☐	16	32

Teacher's notes

Ma2/L2
Operations, relationships between them
Part A

Use the knowledge that subtraction is the inverse of addition

2 marks ☐ ☐

Ma2/L2
Operations, relationships between them
Part B

Understand halving as a way of 'undoing' doubling and vice versa

2 marks ☐ ☐

15.

2 + ☐ = 10

Teacher's notes

Ma2/L2
Mental Methods
Part A

Use mental recall of addition and subtraction facts to 10

1 mark ☐

16.

2 + 4 = 6

so 20 + 40 = ☐

Ma2/L2
Mental Methods
Part A

Use mental recall of addition and subtraction facts to 10

1 mark ☐

---

17. How much money is here?

☐ p

Ma2/L2
Mental Methods
Part B

Use mental calculation strategies to solve number problems including those involving money and measures

1 mark ☐

---

18. A pencil measures 8cm and another pencil measures 8cm. If you put them in a line how much will they measure altogether?

☐ cm

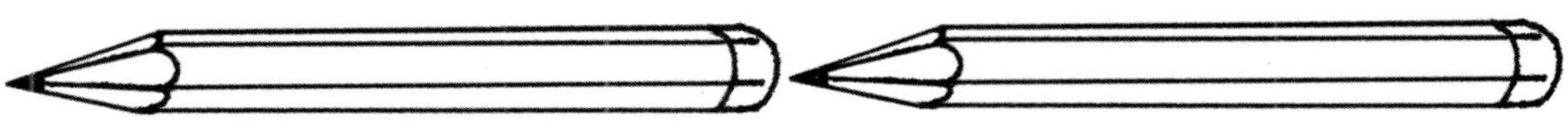

Ma2/L2
Mental Methods
Part B

Use mental calculation strategies to solve number problems including those involving money and measures

1 mark ☐

19. 4 children have 6p each. How much do they have altogether?

[ ] p

Teacher's notes

Ma2/L2
Solving Numerical Problems
Part A

Choose the appropriate operation when solving addition and subtraction problems

1 mark [ ]

---

20. I have 15 books to share between 3 children. How many will they get each?

[ ]

Ma2/L2
Solving Numerical Problems
Part A

Choose the appropriate operation when solving addition and subtraction problems

1 mark [ ]

---

21. If I buy a pencil for 45p and a rubber for 8p, how much do I spend altogether?

[ ] p

Ma2/L2
Solving Numerical Problems
Part B

Solve number problems involving money and measures

1 mark [ ]

---

22. If I have 50p and spend 9p, how much do I have left?

[ ] p

Ma2/L2
Solving Numerical Problems
Part B

Solve number problems involving money and measures

1 mark [ ]

23. There are 30 children in a class. 5 are off sick, so there are only 25 here today.

Choose numbers and symbols to make a number sentence.

30	25	+	-	5	=

---

24. Draw the arrow to the shape.

triangle pyramid prism rectangle square

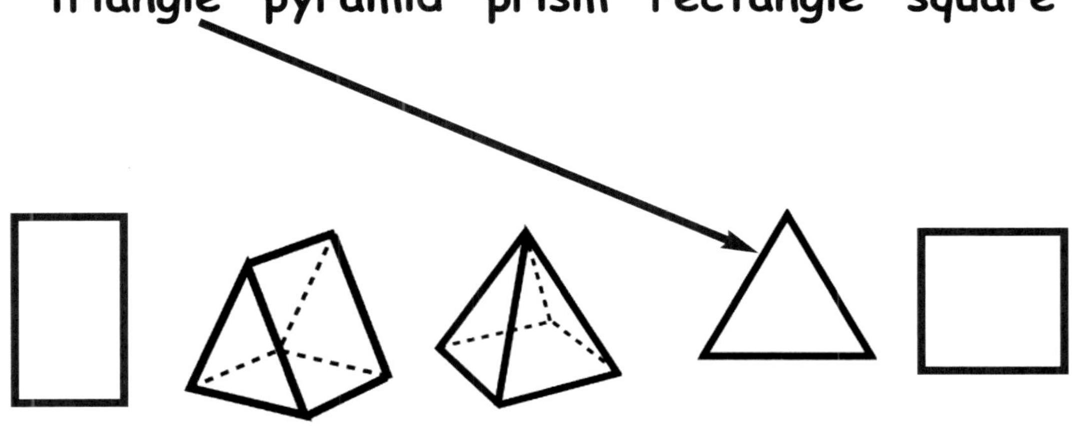

Teacher's notes

Ma2/L2
Written methods
Part A

Record their work in writing

1 mark

Ma3/L2
Properties of Shape
Part A

Use mathematical names for common 3-D and 2-D shapes

1 mark

25. Write the number of sides next to the shape.

Picture of Shape	Number of straight sides
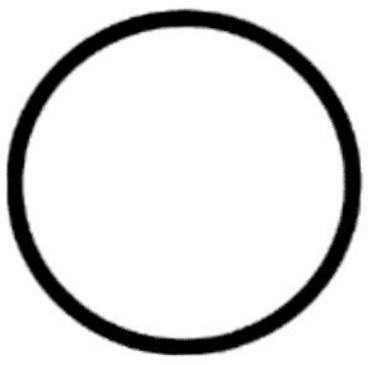	
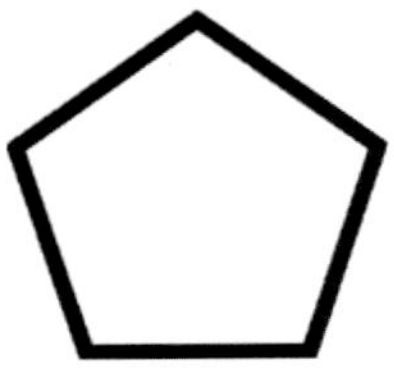	
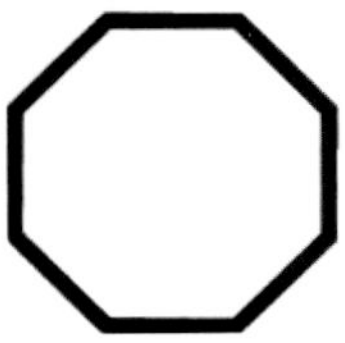	

Teacher's notes

Ma3/L2
Properties of Shape Part B

Describe their properties, including number of sides and corners

1 mark

---

26. Write the number of corners next to the shape.

Picture of Shape	Number of corners
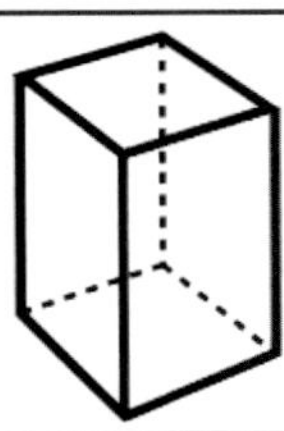	

Ma3/L2
Properties of Shape Part B

Describe their properties, including number of sides and corners

1 mark

27. Draw an arrow to show whether the shape is 2-D or 3-D.

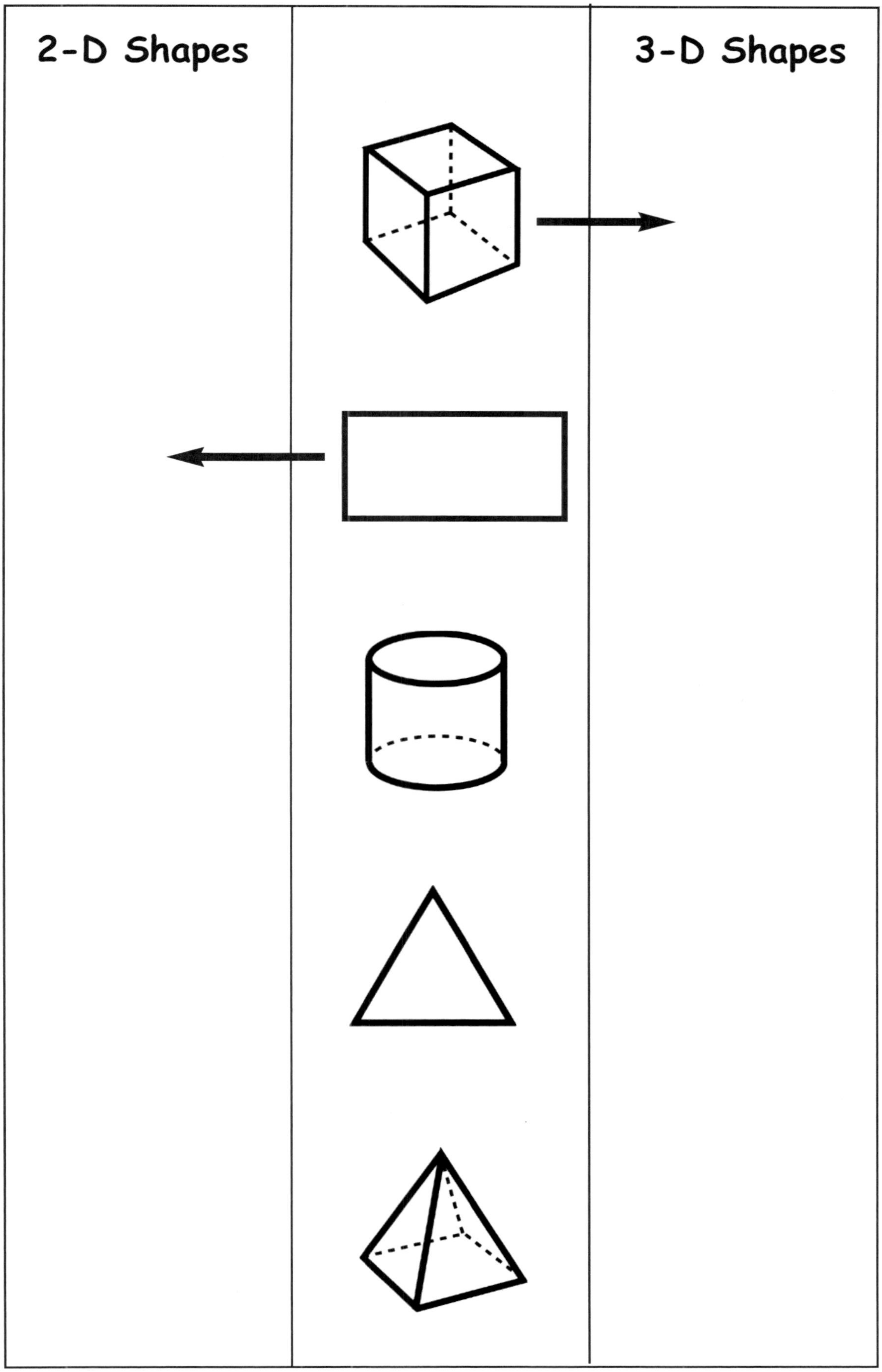

Teacher's notes

Ma3/L2
Properties of Shape
Part B

Describe their properties, including number of sides and corners

1 mark

28. What is the name of the fourth shape?

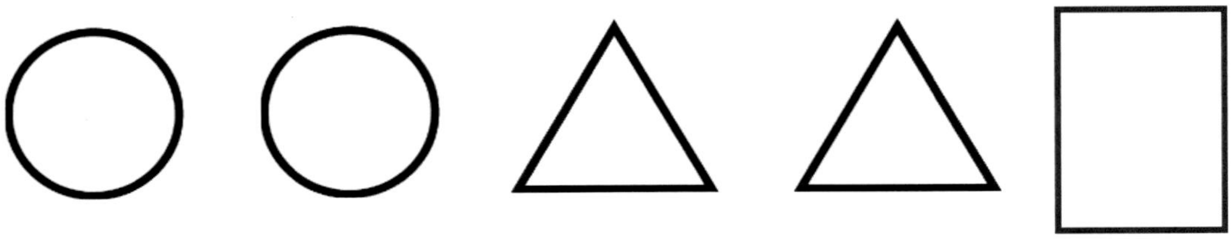

29. Here is an star. Draw another star on the right hand side of it.

30. I face South and turn one right angle clockwise. Where am I facing now?

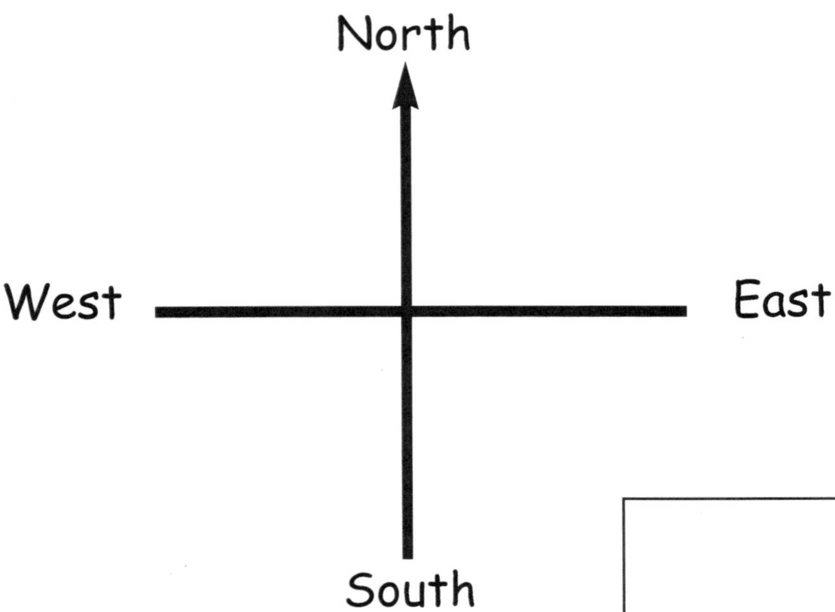

Teacher's notes

Ma3/L2
Properties of position and movement
Part A

Describe the position of objects

1 mark

Ma3/L2
Properties of position and movement
Part B

Distinguish between straight and turning movements

1 mark

Ma3/L2
Properties of position and movement
Part B

Distinguish between straight and turning movements

1 mark

31. Tick the musical notes that have made a quarter turn...

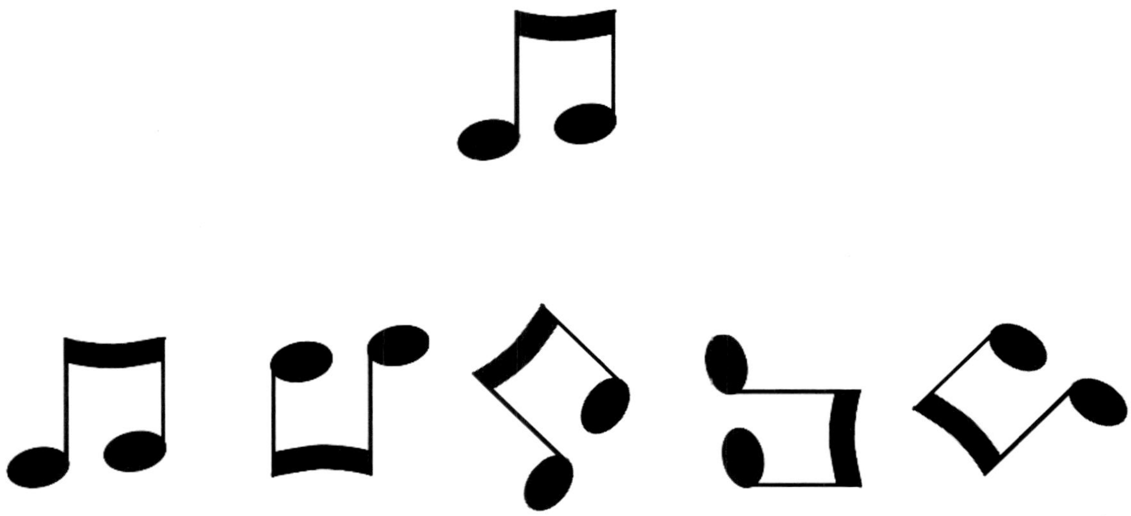

---

32. What would you use to measure the following? Show with arrows.

The height of a room	A ruler
The length of a pencil	A weighing scale
50g of sugar	A metre stick

Teacher's notes

Ma3/L2
Measures
Part A

Understand angle as a measurement of turn – make whole turns, half turns and quarter turns

1 mark

Ma3/L2
Measures
Part B

Begin to use every day non-standard and standard units to measure length and mass

1 mark

33. Put the days of the week in order, starting with Monday.

Friday

~~Monday~~

Tuesday

Wednesday

Saturday

Thursday

1st Monday
2nd
3rd
4th
5th
6th

Teacher's notes

Ma3/L2
Measures
Part C

Begin to use a wider range of measures

1 mark

---

34. Write 'green square' and 'orange square' in the right place on the Carroll diagram.

	Square	**Not Square**
Orange		
Not Orange		

Ma4/L2
Processing and representing data
Part A

Sort objects and classify them using more than one criterion

1 mark

A graph to show the shoe sizes of children in class 1.

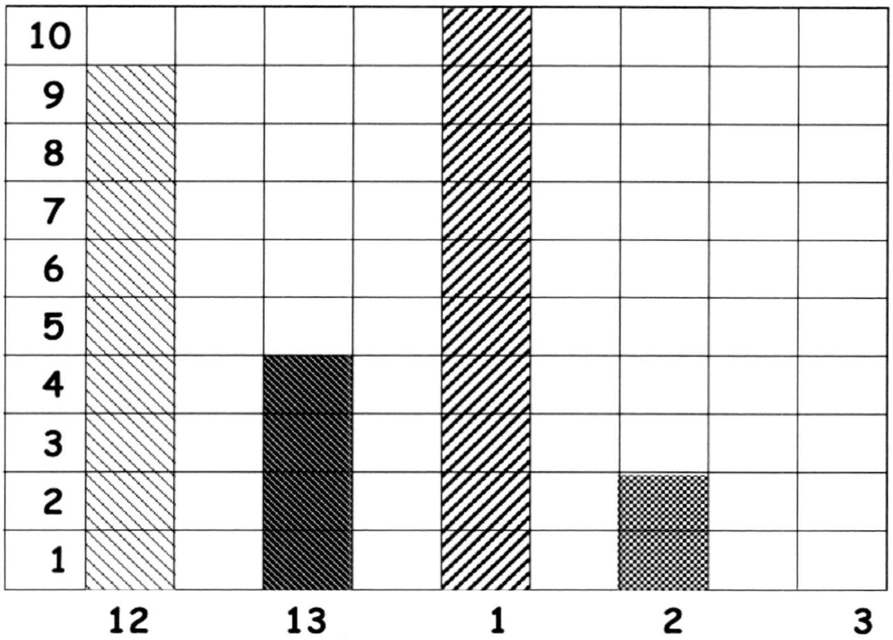

Teacher's notes

35. Which is the most popular shoe size?

Ma4/L2
Processing and representing data
Part B

Understand vocabulary relating to handling data

1 mark

---

36. The graph is not finished.
Here is how many children had size 3 shoes.

How many is this?

Ma4/L2
Processing and representing data
Part C

Collect and sort data to test a simple hypothesis

---

37. Use your answer from question 36 to draw the number of children who had size 3 shoes on the graph above.

Ma4/L2
Processing and representing data
Part D
Record results in simple lists, tables, pictograms and block graphs.

2 marks

---

38. How many children wear size 13 shoes?

Ma4/L2
Interpreting data
Part A

Communicate their findings, using the simple lists, tables, pictograms and block graphs they have recorded

1 mark

Assessing Pupil Progress in Mathematics (APP)

and Identifying Gaps in Pupil's Learning (Year 1 - Level 3)

Name		Date	

This test can be used to confirm a teacher's informal assessment of a pupil. It can also be used to indicate gaps in a pupil's learning.

How to confirm a teacher's informal assessment of a pupil

The test is in two parts. One part consists of an un-timed written paper test for the pupil to complete unaided. The other part (found below) consists of a simple grid for the teacher to complete after observing the pupil in a normal classroom situation. This part of the assessment mainly indicates performance against Attainment Target 1 – Using and Applying Mathematics. The scores for the two tests should be added together and a National Curriculum sub-level awarded using the information in the table at the bottom of this page. The resulting score should give a clear indication of which sub-level the pupil is working at within the levels found in the English National Curriculum.

How to indicate gaps in a pupil's learning

Each question on the written paper is accompanied by the learning objective it represents taken from the tables reproduced at the beginning of the book. By referring to the incorrect questions a list of learning objectives which indicate the gaps in the pupil's learning can quickly and easily be made up.

Teacher Assessment of Attainment Target 1 – Using & Applying (Ma1) and some of Attainment Target 4 – Handling and Data (Ma4) 1 mark indicates some ability 0 mark indicates unable to carry out	**Mark** 0 or 1 for each statement
Ma1/L3 – Problem solving - Part A Select the mathematics they use in a wider range of classroom activities	
Ma1/L3 – Problem solving - Part B Try different approaches	
Ma1/L3 – Problem solving - Part B Find ways of overcoming difficulties that arise when they are solving problems	
Ma1/L3 – Communicating - Part A Begin to organise their work and check results	
Ma1/L3 – Communicating - Part B Discuss their mathematical work and begin to explain their thinking	
Ma1/L3 – Communicating - Part C Use and interpret mathematics symbols and diagrams	
Ma1/L3 – Reasoning - Part A Understand a general statement by finding particular examples that match it	
Ma1/L3 – Reasoning - Part B Review their work and reasoning	
Ma4/L3 – Processing and representing data - Part A Gather information – decide which data to collect	
Ma4/L3 – Processing and representing data - Part B Construct bar charts and pictograms, where the symbol represents a group of units	
Total =	

	Actual	**Possible**
Teacher Assessment of AT1 from above.		10
Paper Test Score		40
Total		50
Sub Level Awarded		

Level 3a high	**= 42 - 50**
Level 3b secure	**= 32 - 41**
Level 3c low	**= 21 - 31**
Below Level 3	**= 20 or less**

1. Put these numbers in order – smallest first.

779	792	709	79	97

2. Round these numbers to the nearest 10.

The nearest 10 to 52 is...

The nearest 10 to 243 is...

3. Tick the coldest place.

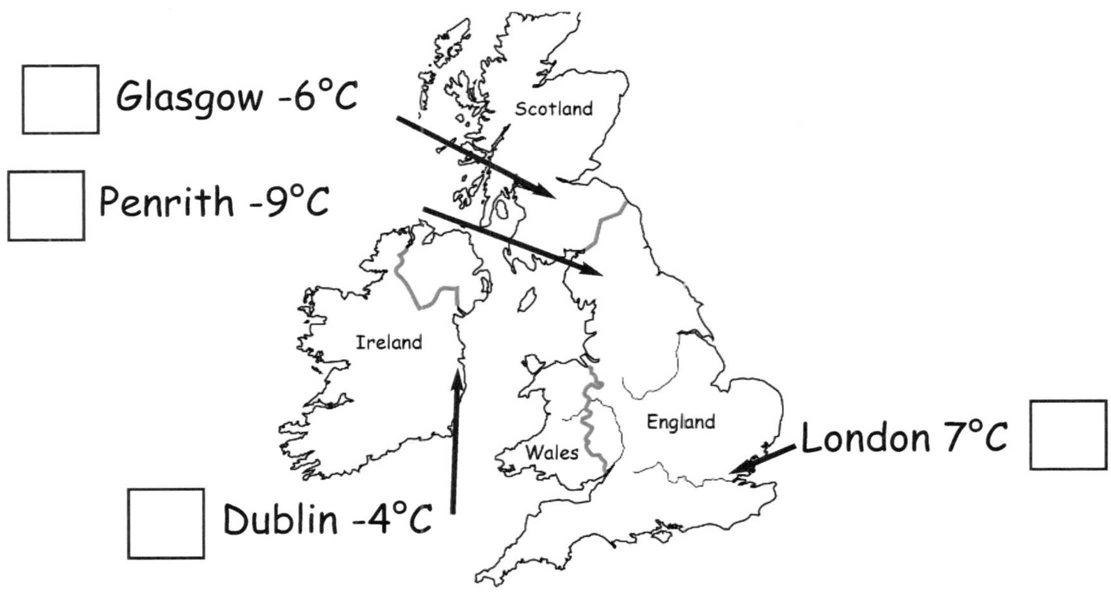

4. What is the difference in temperature between London and Glasgow?

°C

Teacher's notes

Ma2/L3
Numbers and the number system
Part A

Understand place value in numbers to 1000

1 mark

Ma2/L3
Numbers and the number system
Part B

Use place value to make approximations

2 marks

Ma2/L3
Numbers and the number system
Part C

Recognise negative numbers in contexts such as temperature

1 mark

Ma2/L3
Numbers and the number system
Part C

Recognise negative numbers in contexts such as temperature

1 mark

Teacher's notes

5. Write in the missing numbers.

	+5		+5		+5		+5	
21	→		→	31	→		→	41

Ma2/L3
Numbers and the number system
Part D

Recognise a wider range of sequences

1 mark

---

6. Write in the next number in the sequence.

7	14	21	28	

Ma2/L3
Numbers and the number system
Part D

Recognise a wider range of sequences

1 mark

---

7. Callum has 90p. He spends $\frac{1}{3}$.
How much does he have left?

p

Ma2/L3
Fractions and decimals
Part A

Use simple fractions that are several parts of a whole and recognise when two simple fractions are equivalent

1 mark

8. Circle the fractions that are equal to $\frac{1}{3}$?

$\frac{3}{7}$ $\frac{2}{6}$ $\frac{10}{30}$ $\frac{1}{30}$

Teacher's notes

Ma2/L3
Fractions and decimals
Part A

Use simple fractions that are several parts of a whole and recognise when two simple fractions are equivalent

1 mark

---

9. Bethan buys a book for £2.45 and a pencil for 63p. How much does she spend altogether?

£ ☐

Ma2/L3
Fractions and decimals
Part B

Begin to use decimal notation in contexts such as money

1 mark

10.

23 × 8 = 184

so 184 ÷ 23 = ☐

Ma2/L3
Operations, relationships between them
Part A

Derive associated division facts from known multiplication facts

1 mark

11.

17 + 5 = 12 + ☐

Ma2/L3
Operations, relationships between them
Part B

Begin to understand the role of '=', the 'equals' sign

1 mark

12.

49 + 34 = ☐

13.

80 - 35 = ☐

14.

☐ × ☐ = 40

☐ × ☐ = 14

---

15. Nathan has 80p. He spends $\frac{1}{4}$.
How much does he spend?

☐ p

Teacher's notes

Ma2/L3
Mental Methods
Part A

Add and Subtract two-digit numbers mentally

1 mark ☐

Ma2/L3
Mental Methods
Part A

Add and Subtract two-digit numbers mentally

1 mark ☐

Ma2/L3
Mental Methods
Part B

Use mental recall of the 2, 3, 4, 5 and 10 multiplication tables

2 marks ☐ ☐

Ma2/L3
Mental Methods
Part B

Use mental recall of the 2, 3, 4, 5 and 10 multiplication tables

1 mark ☐

16. Olivia has 90p. She buys a pear for 25p and a banana for 35p. How much does she have left?

[ ] p

Teacher's notes

Ma2/L3
Solving numerical problems
Part A

Use mental recall of addition and subtraction facts to 20 in solving problems involving larger numbers

1 mark [ ]

---

17. 6 children share out a bag of sweets. Each child gets 5 sweets and there are 2 sweets left over. How many sweets were in the bag?

[ ] sweets

Ma2/L3
Solving numerical problems
Part B

Solve whole number problems including those involving multiplication or division that may give rise to remainders

1 mark [ ]

---

18. Bananas are sold in bags of 7.
How many bananas are there in 4 bags?

[ ] bananas

Ma2/L3
Solving numerical problems
Part B

Solve whole number problems including those involving multiplication or division that may give rise to remainders

1 mark [ ]

19.

236 + 337 = [ ]

Ma2/L3
Written Methods
Part A

Add and subtract three-digit numbers using written method

1 mark [ ]

20.

740 - 329 = ☐

Teacher's notes

Ma2/L3
Written Methods
Part A

Add and subtract three-digit numbers using written method

1 mark ☐

21.

What is 17 x 5 = ☐

Ma2/L3
Written Methods
Part B

Multiply and divide two-digit numbers by 2, 3, 4 and 5 as well as 10 with whole number answers and remainders

1 mark ☐

---

22. Tick the divisions that have an answer of 5.

50 ÷ 10 =	30 ÷ 3 =
20 ÷ 4 =	18 ÷ 2 =

Ma2/L3
Written Methods
Part B

Multiply and divide two-digit numbers by 2, 3, 4 and 5 as well as 10 with whole number answers and remainders

1 mark ☐

---

23. Tick the divisions that have a remainder of 2.

27 ÷ 5 =	12 ÷ 5 =
23 ÷ 5 =	33 ÷ 5 =

Ma2/L3
Written Methods
Part B

Multiply and divide two-digit numbers by 2, 3, 4 and 5 as well as 10 with whole number answers and remainders

1 mark ☐

24. Write the number of right-angles in each shape.

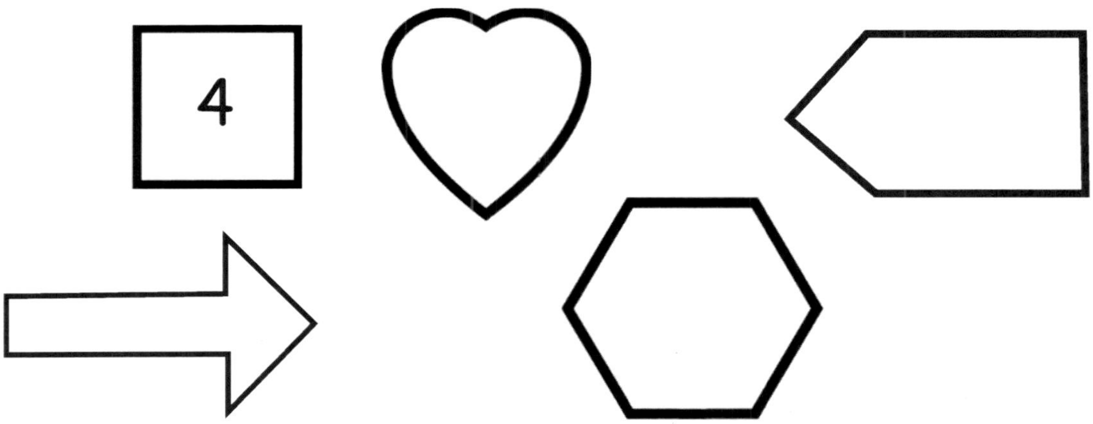

Teacher's notes

Ma3/L3
Properties of shape
Part A

Classify 3-D and 2-D shapes in various ways using mathematical properties such as reflective symmetry for 2-D shapes

1 mark

---

25. Put a circle around the equilateral triangle.

Ma3/L3
Properties of shape
Part A

Classify 3-D and 2-D shapes in various ways using mathematical properties such as reflective symmetry for 2-D shapes

1 mark

---

26. Tick the triangular prism.

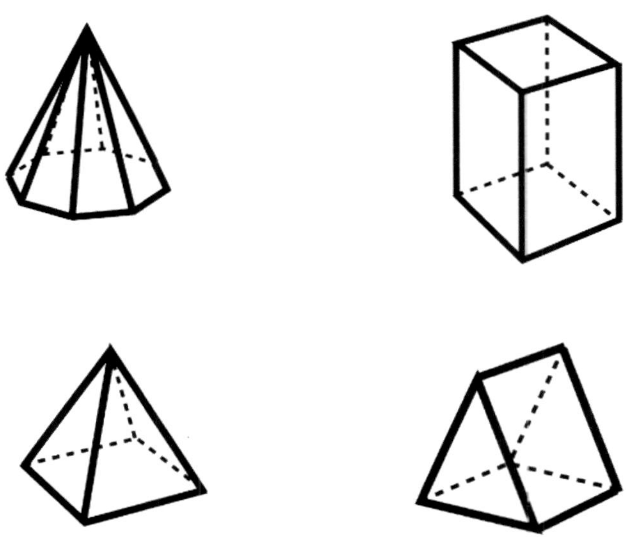

Ma3/L3
Properties of shape
Part A

Classify 3-D and 2-D shapes in various ways using mathematical properties such as reflective symmetry for 2-D shapes

1 mark

27. Put a cross on the nets which will **not** make a cube.

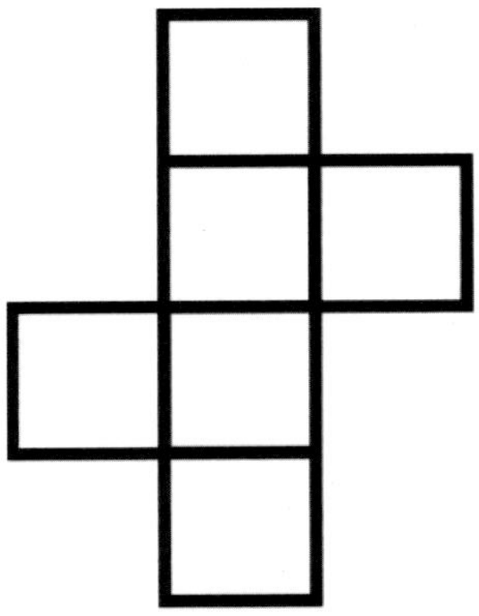

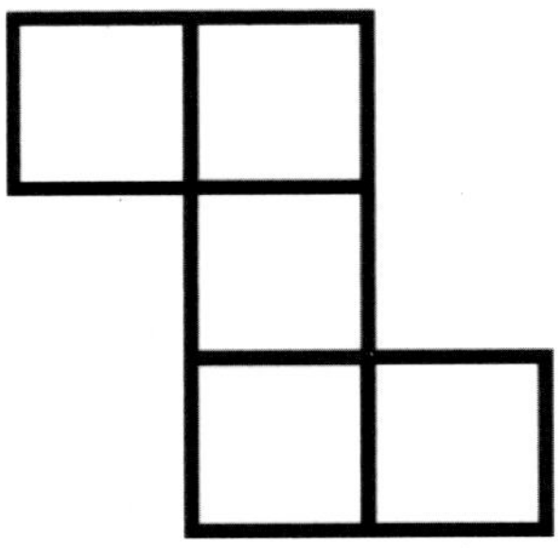

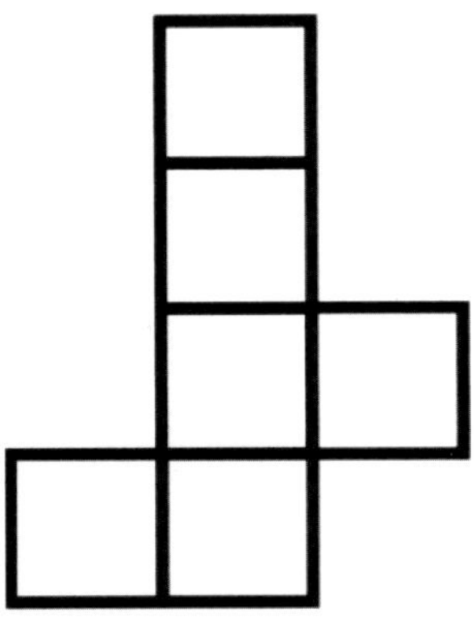

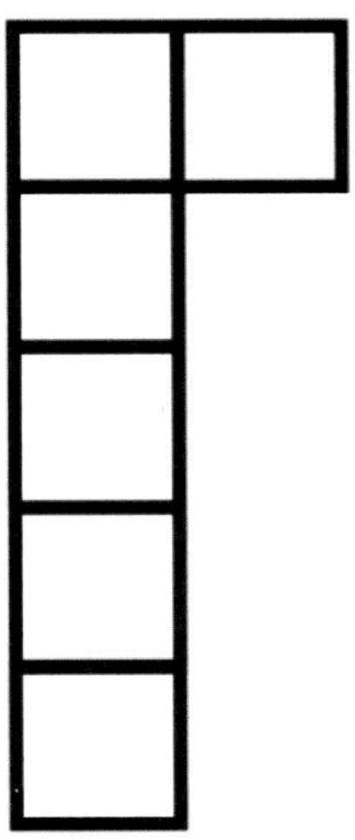

Teacher's notes

Ma3/L3
Properties of shape Part B

Begin to recognise nets of familiar 3-D shapes

1 mark

28. What is the name of this shape?

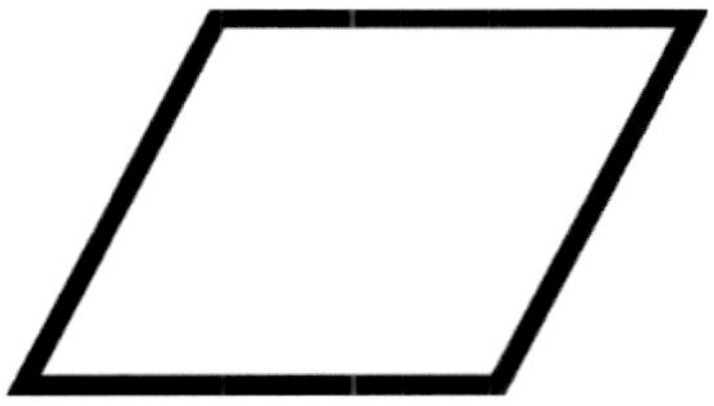

It is a...

---

29. Reflect the pattern in the mirror line.

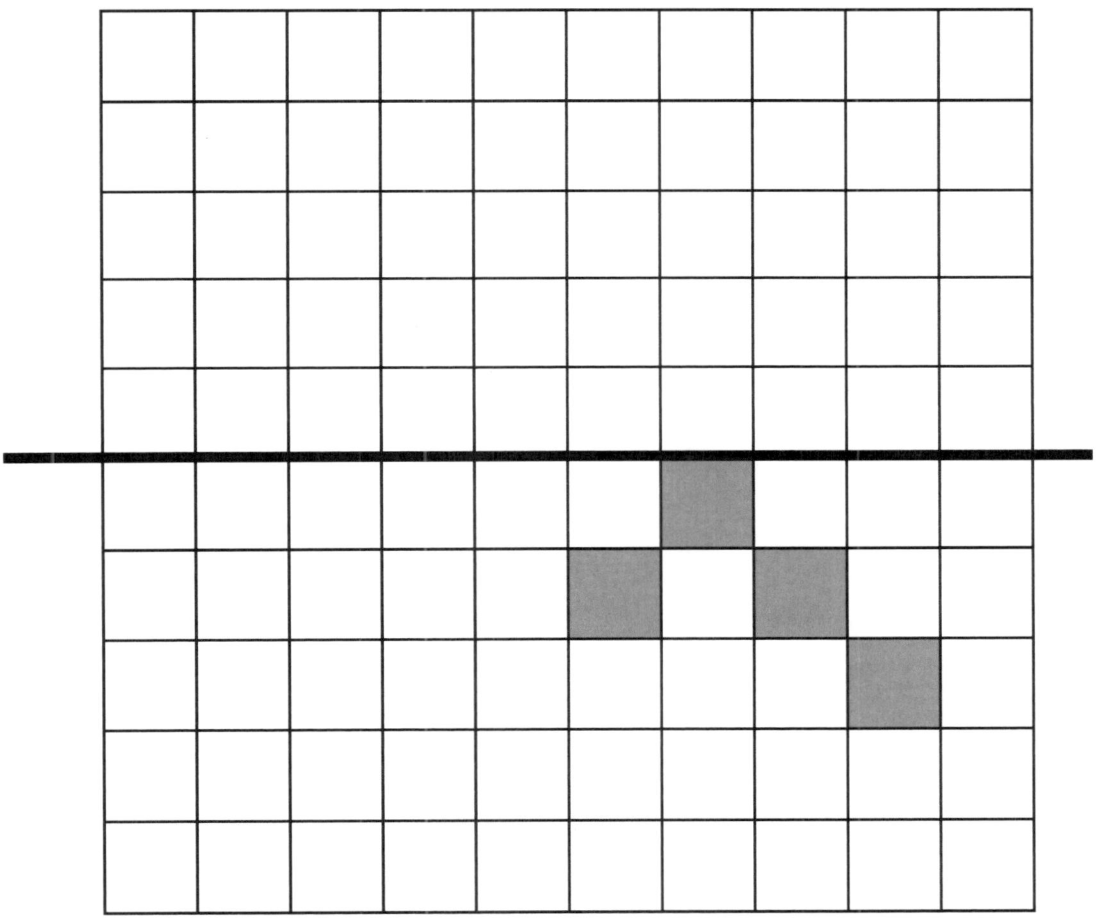

Teacher's notes

Ma3/L3
Properties of position and movement Part A

Recognise shapes in different orientations

1 mark

Ma3/L3
Properties of position and movement Part B

Reflect shapes presented on a grid, in a vertical or horizontal mirror line

1 mark

30. Tick the correct word.

start

finish

The shape above has been rotated 90°.
Which way has it been rotated?

clockwise ☐ anticlockwise ☐

Teacher's notes

Ma3/L3
Properties of position and movement
Part C

Describe position and movement

1 mark ☐

---

31. How long is this line?

☐ cm

Ma3/L3
Measures
Part A

Use non-standard units and standard metric units of length, capacity and mass in a range of contexts

1 mark ☐

---

32. How long is a lesson that starts at 10.20am and finishes at 10.45am?

☐ minutes

Ma3/L3
Measures
Part B

Use standard units of time

1 mark ☐

---

33. How many degrees make a whole turn?

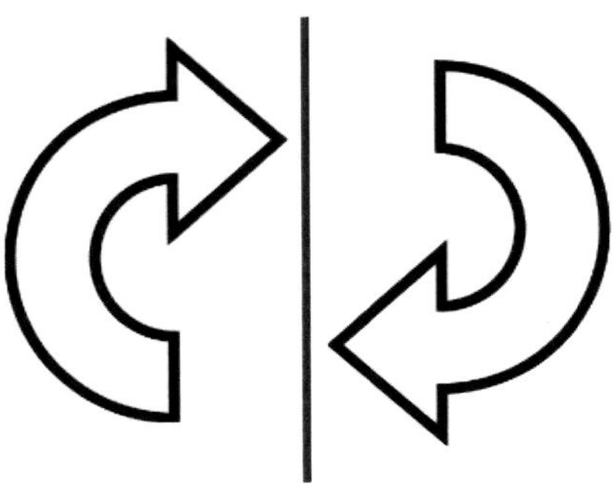

☐ o

Ma3/L3
Measures
Part C

Use a wider range of measures

1 mark ☐

34. Copy these two shapes onto the Carroll diagram below.

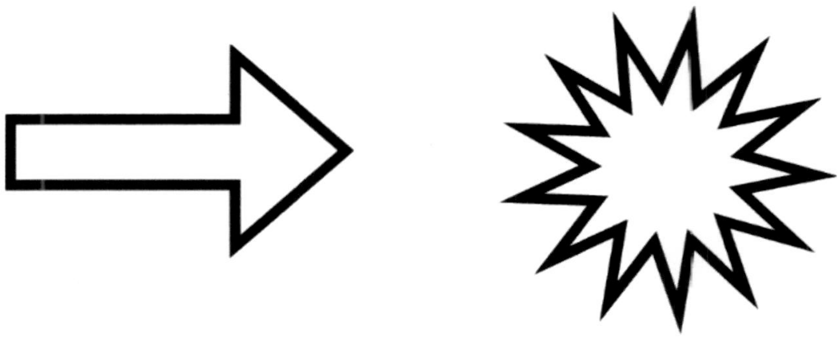

	Right Angles	No Right Angles
A line of symmetry		
No line of symmetry		

Teacher's notes

Ma4/L3
Processing and representing data
Parts A and B

(See Teacher Assessment on the first page of this test paper.)

Ma4/L3
Processing and representing data
Part C

Use Venn and Carroll diagrams to record their sorting and classifying of information

2 marks

Graph to show the favourite subject of children in a school.

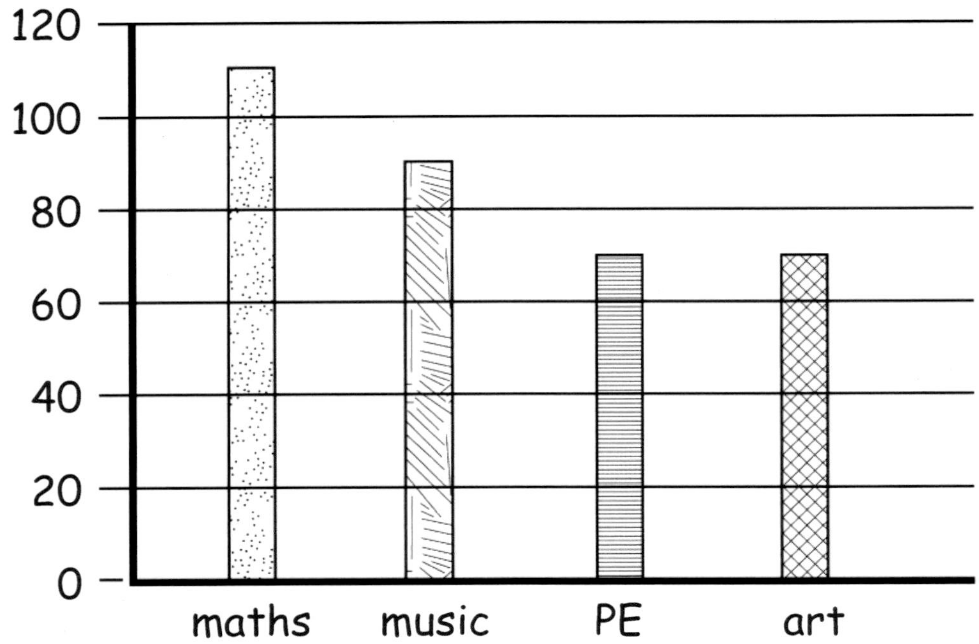

35. How many children in the school like maths?

children

36. How many more children like music than PE?

children

37. How many children took part in this survey?

children

Teacher's notes

Ma4/L3
Interpreting data
Part A

Extract and interpret information presented in simple tables, lists, bar charts and pictograms

3 marks

Answers **Year 1 - Level 2**

1 12

2 81

3 19

4 46, 56

5 12, 6, 2, 40, 0

6 8

7 4

8 6

9 3

10 e.g.

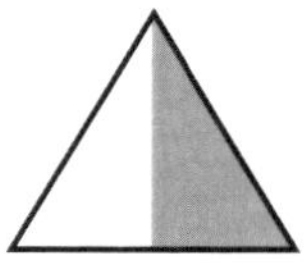

11 e.g. 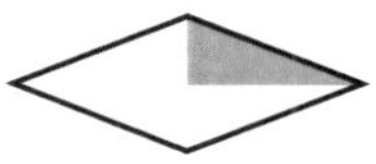

12 6

13 18 - 10 = 8   18 - 8 = 10

14

Half		Double
2	4	8
5	10	**20**
6	12	**24**
8	16	32

15 8

16 60

17 100p

18 16cm

19 24p

20 5

21 53p

22 41p

23 30 - 5 = 25

24 *triangle*  *pyramid* 

prism  *rectangle* 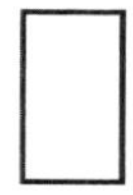

square 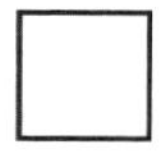

25 0, 5, 8

26 8, 5, 6

27 *3D Shapes*  

2D Shapes 

28 triangle

29

30 west

31 

32 *The length of a pencil.....*A ruler
*50g of sugar.....*A weighing scale

33 *2nd* Tuesday
3rd Wednesday
4th Thursday
5th Friday
6th Saturday

34 *Orange / Square* ..... orange square
Not Orange / Square ..... green square

35 1

36 7

37

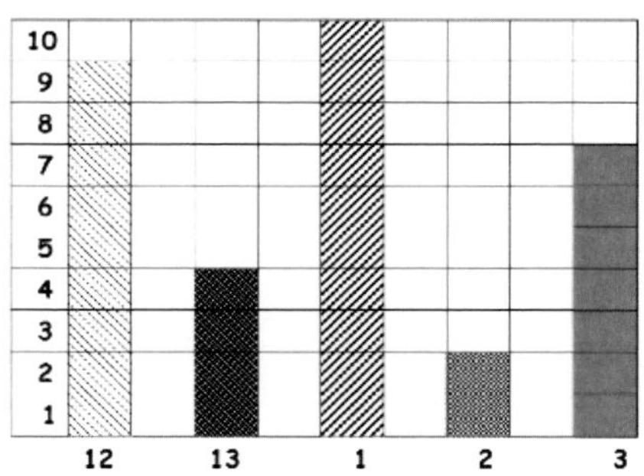

38 4

Answers **Year 1 - Level 3**

1 79, 97, 709, 779, 792

2 50, 240

3 Penrith -9°C

4 13°C

5 26, 36

6 35

7 60p

8 $\frac{2}{6}$ $\frac{10}{30}$

9 £3.08

10 8

11 10

12 83

13 45

14 e.g. 4 x 10 = 40 2 x 7 = 14

15 20p

16 30p

17 32 sweets

18 28 bananas

19 573

20 411

21 85

22 50 ÷ 10 = 20 ÷ 4 =

23 27 ÷ 5 = 12 ÷ 5 =

24
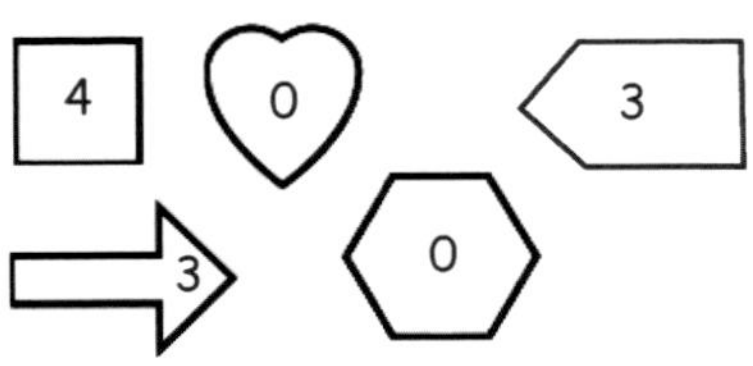

25

26

27
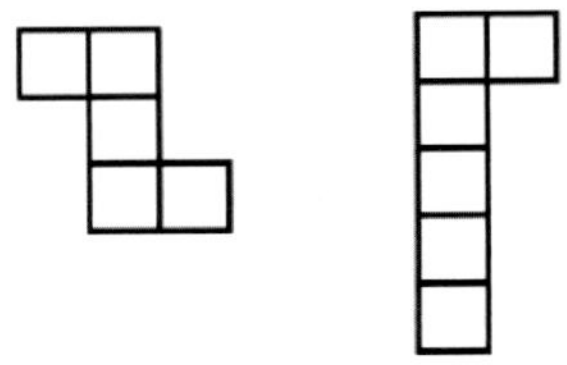

28 rhombus

29
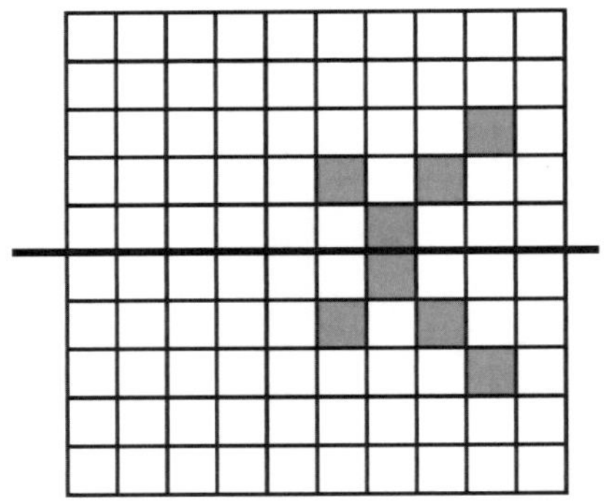

30 anticlockwise

31 6cm

32 25 minutes

33 360°

34

	Right Angles	No Right Angles
A line of symmetry	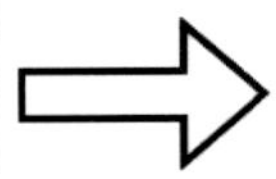	
No line of symmetry		

35 110 children

36 20 children

37 340 children

APP Year 1 Level 1 **Date:** **Group:**

		Names																
	Qu.1	Estimate and check a number to 10																
	Qu.2	Estimate and check a number to 10																
	Qu.3	Read and write numbers to 10																
	Qu.4	Say what number comes next to 10																
	Qu.5	Say what number is one more to 10																
	Qu.6	Say what number is one less within 10																
	Qu.7	Count back to 0 from 10																
	Qu.8	Place 1 – 10 in ascending order																
	Qu.9	Point to 1st, 2nd etc in a line																
	Qu.10	Begin to count in twos to 10																
	Qu.11	Halve paper shapes and lengths of string																
MA2	Qu.12	Half fill containers of water																
	Qu.13	Half an even number of objects																
	Qu.14	Find the total of two or more sets of objects																
	Qu.15	Take objects from a set / how many left																
	Qu.16	Add by counting on																
	Qu.17	Know doubles of numbers to double 5																
	Qu.18	Given a number, how many more make…																
	Qu.19	Which pairs add up to a given total																
	Qu.20	How many balance with…																
	Qu.21	Solve problems involving 1p or £1 coins																
	Qu.22	Record work with pictures or diagrams																
	Qu.23	Begin to use the symbols '+' and ' = '																
	Qu.24	Sort shapes and say how selected																
	Qu.25	Describe properties of 2-D and 3-D shapes																
	Qu.26	Refer to sides and corners of shapes																
	Qu.27	Name the shapes they use																
	Qu.28	Respond to / use positional language																
	Qu.29	Respond to / use directional language																
MA3	Qu.30	Compare lengths and put in order																
	Qu.31	Use language of comparison e.g. longer																
	Qu.32	Order 3 heavier / lighter objects																
	Qu.33	Compare with a metre or 500g or 1 litre																
	Qu.34	Order everyday events																
	Qu.35	Use the vocabulary of days of the week																
	Qu.36	Read analogue hour and half hour																
	Qu.37	Sort using simple criteria																
	Qu.38	Sort using a different criteria																
	Qu.39	Respond to questions about own sorting																
	Qu.40	Demonstrate criteria used for sorting																
MA4	Qu.41	Talk about how they represented sorting																
	Qu.42	Sort using Venn or Carroll diagram																
	Qu.43	Sort using Venn or Carroll diagram																
	Qu.44	Make simple block graphs with objects																
	Qu.45	Use sorted objects as a record																

APP Mathematics - Gap analysis for group and individual target setting

APP Year 1 Level 2 **Date:** **Group:**

		Names															
	Qu.1	Count sets of objects reliably															
	Qu.2	Order numbers up to 100															
	Qu.3	Order numbers up to 100															
	Qu.4	Recognise sequences of numbers															
	Qu.5	Recognise sequences of numbers															
	Qu.6	Begin to use halves and quarters															
	Qu.7	Begin to use halves and quarters															
	Qu.8	Begin to use halves and quarters															
	Qu.9	Begin to use halves and quarters															
	Qu.10	Explore concept of half of a shape															
	Qu.11	Explore concept of half of a shape															
MA2	Qu.12	Use subtraction as the inverse of addition															
	Qu.13	Use subtraction as the inverse of addition															
	Qu.14	Use halving to 'undo' doubling & vice versa															
	Qu.15	Use addition and subtraction facts to 10															
	Qu.16	Use addition and subtraction facts to 10															
	Qu.17	Solve problems mentally involving money															
	Qu.18	Solve problems mentally involving measure															
	Qu.19	Choose appropriate operation solving problems															
	Qu.20	Choose appropriate operation solving problems															
	Qu.21	Solve problems involving money and measures															
	Qu.22	Solve problems involving money and measures															
	Qu.23	Record number work in writing															
	Qu.24	Name common 2D and 3D shapes															
	Qu.25	Describe shape properties e.g sides/corners															
	Qu.26	Describe shape properties e.g sides/corners															
	Qu.27	Describe shape properties e.g sides/corners															
MA3	Qu.28	Describe the position of objects															
	Qu.29	Distinguish between straight/turning movements															
	Qu.30	Distinguish between straight/turning movements															
	Qu.31	Make whole/ half/ quarter turns															
	Qu.32	Use units to measure length and mass															
	Qu.33	Begin to use days of the week/ other measures															
	Qu.34	Sort/classify using more than one criterion															
	Qu.35	Understand vocabulary relating to data															
MA4	Qu.36	Collect, sort and test data															
	Qu.37	Record results in block graphs															
	Qu.38	Communicate findings using block graphs															